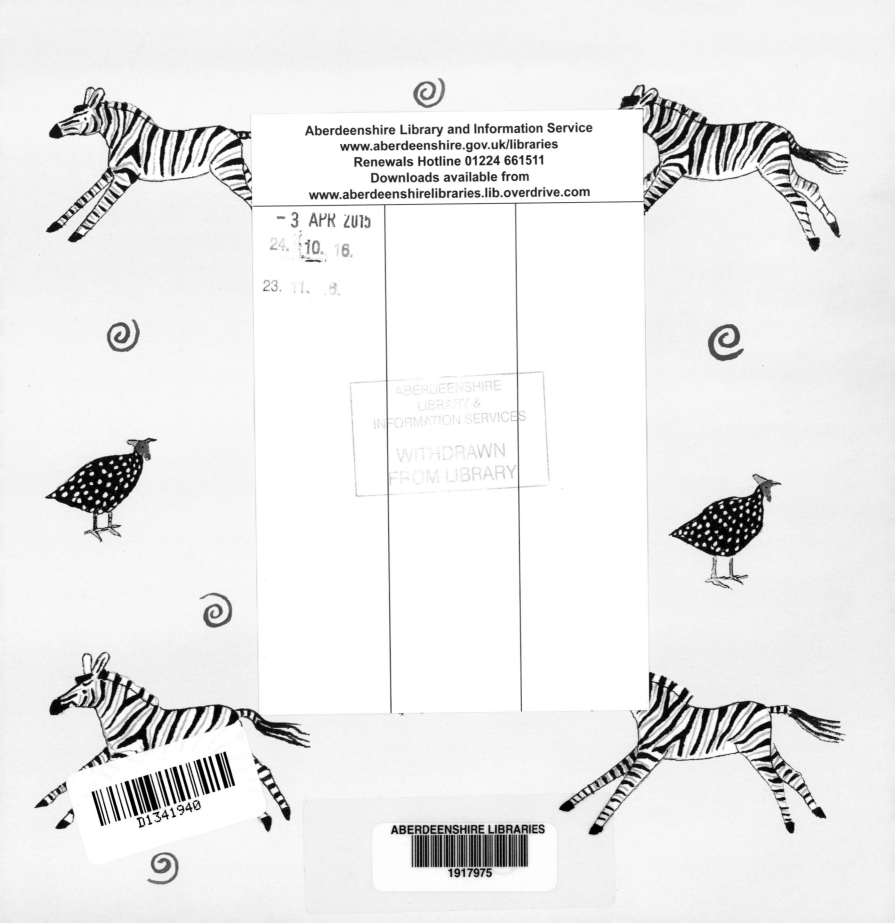

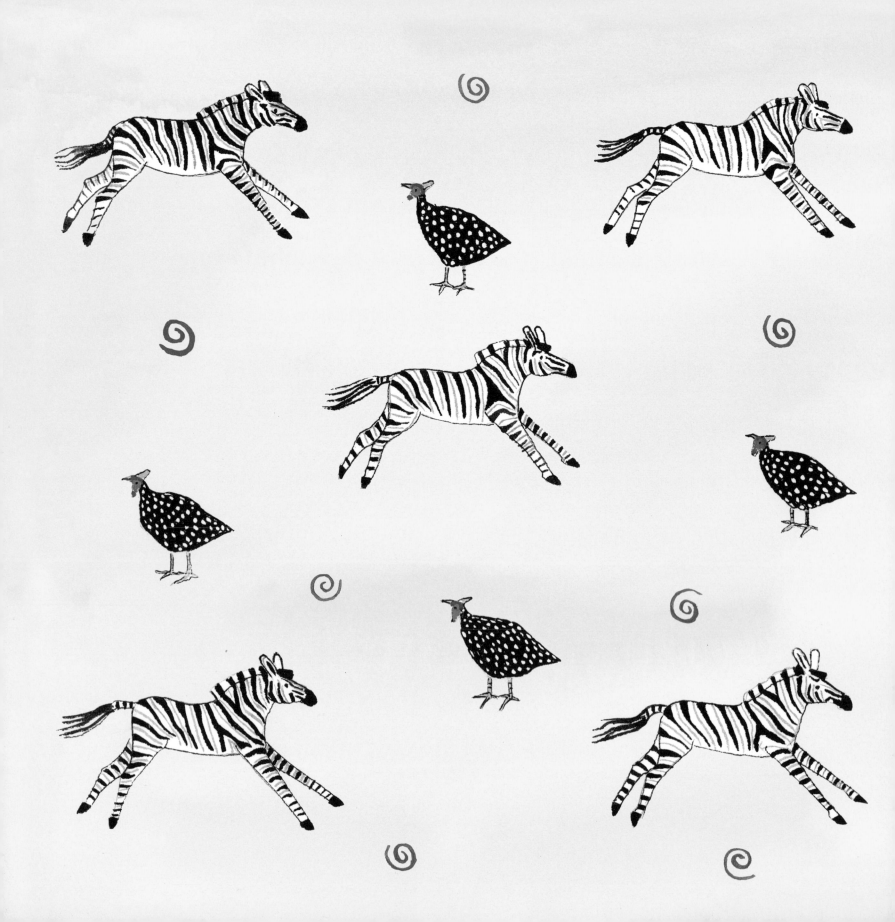

We All Went on Safari

A Counting Journey through Tanzania

For my grandsons – Tim, Gibson, Billy, Joe, Bennett –
and for the children of Farmingville Elementary School – L. K.

For Helen and Lucy, with love – J. C.

Barefoot Books would like to thank Dr. Michael Sheridan,
Visiting Assistant Professor of Sociology and Anthropology at Middlebury College, Vermont,
for his kind help with Swahili translation and pronunciation

Barefoot Books
124 Walcot Street
Bath
BA1 5BG

First published in Great Britain in 2003 by Barefoot Books, Ltd

This book was typeset in Legacy
The illustrations were prepared in watercolour

Graphic design by Louise Millar, London
Colour separation by Grafiscan, Verona
Printed and bound in China by Printplus Ltd.

This book has been printed on 100% acid-free paper

ISBN 1-84148-457-1

British Library Cataloguing-in-Publication Data:
A catalogue record for this book is available from the British Library

5 7 9 8 6 4

We All Went on Safari

A Counting Journey through Tanzania

Written by Laurie Krebs
Illustrated by Julia Cairns

Barefoot Books
Celebrating Art and Story

We all went on safari,
When the day had just begun.

We spied a lonely leopard.
Arusha counted one.

moja 1

We all went on safari,
Over grasslands damp with dew.

We came across some ostriches,
And Mosi counted two.

mbili **2**

We all went on safari,
Past an old acacia tree.

Nearby giraffes were grazing,
So Tumpe counted three.

tatu **3**

We all went on safari,
To the ancient crater floor.

We heard some lordly lions.
Mwambe counted four.

nne **4**

We all went on safari,
Where the lake birds swim and dive.

Up bobbed some hefty hippos.
Akeyla counted five.

tano **5**

We all went on safari,
Among herds that intermix.

We followed woolly wildebeests.
Watende counted six.

sita **6**

We all went on safari,
With the sun high in the heaven.

We spotted zigzag zebras.
Zalira counted seven.

saba 7

We all went on safari,
Near the Serengeti gate.

We startled wiry warthogs.
Suhuba counted eight.

nane

8

We all went on safari,
Where the treetops intertwine.

We met mischievous monkeys,
So Doto counted nine.

tisa 9

We all went on safari,
Through a rocky hillside glen.

We watched enormous elephants,
And Bodru counted ten.

kumi 10

We all went on safari,
In the sunset's fading light.

We built ourselves a campfire
And bid our friends 'Good night'.

Animals of Tanzania

Leopard – chui *(choo-ee)*
Leopards often carry their prey to a high tree branch, where they can eat and sleep safely. Only their long, spotted tails give away their secret hiding place.

Lion – simba *(sihm-bah)*
The female lion hunts for the pride, which often has up to thirteen family members.

Ostrich – mbuni *(m-boo-nee)*
Ostriches are taller than most professional basketball players, about 7-8 feet, and they are very fast runners!

Hippopotamus – kiboko *(kee-bo-ko)*
Hippos sink down in the water during the day, folding their ears and closing their nostrils, to protect their skin from drying out in the sun.

Giraffe – twiga *(twee-gah)*
Giraffes have long, 18-inch tongues and spongy upper lips that allow them to eat around the spiky thorns of their favourite food, the acacia tree.

Common Wildebeest –
nyumbu (*nyuhm-boo*)

A wildebeest looks like a combination of many different animals. It has the head of an ox, the mane of a horse, the horns of a buffalo and the beard of a goat.

Plains Zebra – punda milia (*pun-dah mee-lee-ah*)

Like humans have fingerprints, each zebra has its own special black and white pattern that helps to camouflage it at dawn and dusk, when lions are hunting.

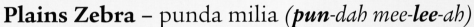

Warthog – ngiri (*ngee-ree*)

Warthog families trot rapidly in single file – mother first and piglets behind – each with its tail straight up in the air.

Vervet Monkey –
umbili (*tuhm-bee-lee*)

Vervet monkey babies hitchhike rides on their mother's chest by holding into her fur and curling their tails round her back.

Elephant –
tembo (*tem-bo*)

A mother elephant cares for her baby with surprising tenderness, keeping it hidden beneath her legs or tucked inside the group when the herd is on the move.

The Maasai People

The Maasai people of East Africa live where northern Tanzania meets southern Kenya. Several families cluster together in small villages. They build their huts of mud, sticks, grass and cow dung. Together they care for a large herd of cattle, the tribe's most important activity. When grazing is good and the pastures rich, the people stay in the settlement. When the land dries out and the seasons change, the group moves on to find fresh water and new pastures for the cattle.

The Maasai are a proud people. Standing tall and handsome in their cloaks of rich red fabric, men and women adorn themselves with beautiful beaded earrings and necklaces. Some men have fancy hairstyles and wear elaborate head-dresses. The women usually shave their heads and wear wide, white, circular collars that bounce rhythmically as they move.

For thousands of years the Maasai have lived amidst the wildlife of East Africa. But in today's rapidly changing world, they are struggling to preserve their way of life as one of the last pastoral cultures on earth.

Swahili Names

When Tanzanian parents choose a name for their child, they often pick a name that has special meaning. They hope their baby will grow up to have the same qualities as the name suggests.

ARUSHA (f) *(ah-**roo**-shah)* – independent, creative, ambitious

WATENDE (m) *(wah-**ten**-day)* – sensitive, generous, creative

MOSI (m) *(**mo**-see)* – patient, responsible, loves his family and home

ZALIRA (f) *(zah-**lee**-rah)* – understanding, peaceful, friendly

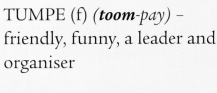

TUMPE (f) *(**toom**-pay)* – friendly, funny, a leader and organiser

SUHUBA (m) *(soo-**hoo**-bah)* – clever, talented, affectionate

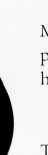

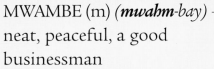

MWAMBE (m) *(**mwahm**-bay)* – neat, peaceful, a good businessman

DOTO (m/f) *(**do**-to)* – generous, affectionate, helpful

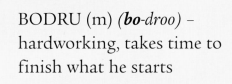

AKEYLA (f) *(ah-**kay**-lah)* – loves nature and the outdoors

BODRU (m) *(**bo**-droo)* – hardworking, takes time to finish what he starts

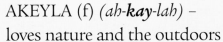

Facts about Tanzania

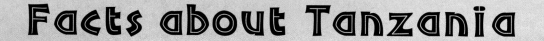

Tanzania is the largest country in East Africa. It is almost as big as France.

Mount Kilimanjaro is the highest mountain in Africa. It is 19,340 feet (5,895 metres) high.

Lake Victoria, in the north, is the second largest lake in the world.

Before 1961, the country was called Tanganyika. One of the big lakes still bears that name, Lake Tanganyika. Now Tanzania is made up of Tanganyika and the island of Zanzibar.

More than 100 tribes live in Tanzania.

The name Serengeti means 'endless plain'.

Ngorongoro Crater is a collapsed volcano. Once it stood taller than Mount Kilimanjaro. Now it is shaped like a deep bowl.

Olduvai Gorge is sometimes called the cradle of mankind. The bones of ancient man were found there.

Counting in Swahili

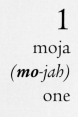

1		**6**	
moja		sita	
(**mo**-jah)		(**see**-tah)	
one		six	
2		**7**	
mbili		saba	
(m-**bee**-lee)		(**sah**-bah)	
two		seven	
3		**8**	
tatu		nane	
(**ta**-too)		(**nah**-nay)	
three		eight	
4		**9**	
nne		tisa	
(**n**-nay)		(**tee**-sah)	
four		nine	
5		**10**	
tano		kumi	
(**tah**-no)		(**koo**-mee)	
five		ten	

Barefoot Books
Celebrating Art and Story

At Barefoot Books, we celebrate art and story with books
that open the hearts and minds of children from all walks of life,
inspiring them to read deeper, search further, and explore
their own creative gifts. Taking our inspiration from many
different cultures, we focus on themes that encourage
independence of spirit, enthusiasm for learning, and
acceptance of other traditions. Thoughtfully prepared
by writers, artists and storytellers from all over the world,
our products combine the best of the present with the best of
the past to educate our children as the caretakers of tomorrow.

www.barefootbooks.com

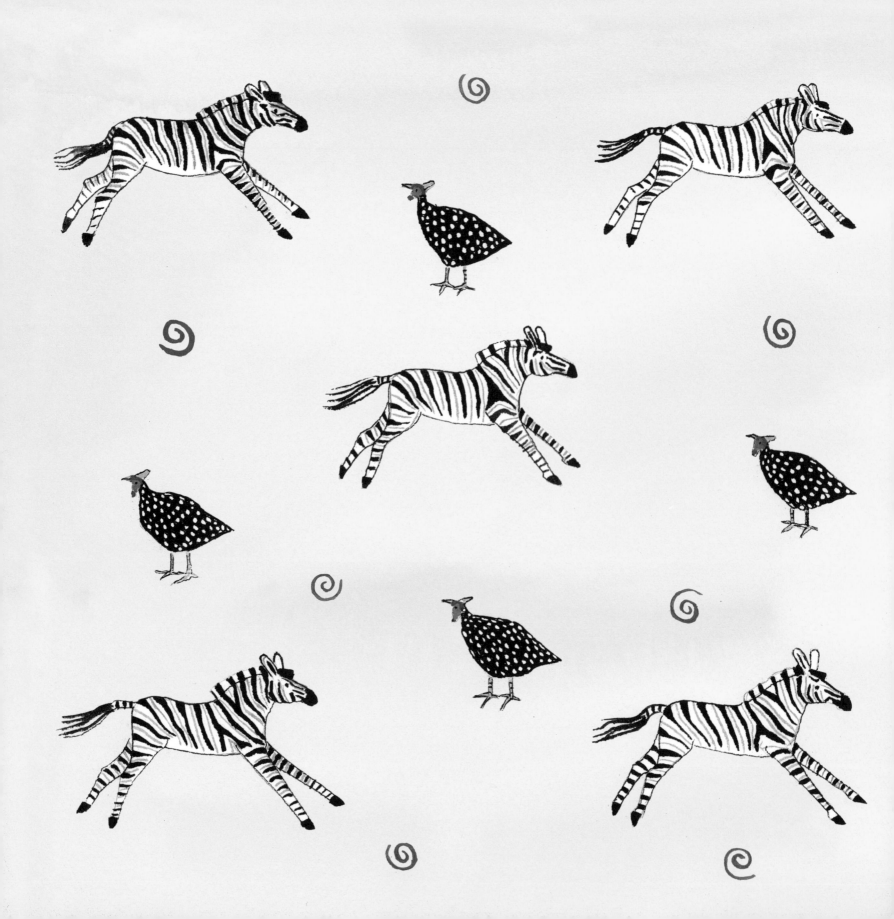